The Father I Thought I'd Be

The Hidden Reality Behind the First Three Months of Fatherhood

Long Dao

This is a work of nonfiction memoir. Names, details, and identifying characteristics of some individuals may have been changed to protect privacy.

Paperback edition

ISBN: 979-8-234-03089-4

Manufactured in the United States of America

Dedicated to my extraordinary wife and two remarkable girls.

I promise to do my best to live in the moments that are the best of us. You three will forever be my heart and soul.

Contents

Introduction

The Father I Thought I Would Be

Before Nora was born, I imagined fatherhood would feel like becoming the man strong enough to hold the world on his shoulders. Like Atlas in the old myths—steady, unshakeable, carrying the weight of everything for the people he loved. I believed love would unlock a strength I didn't yet possess, something immovable and inexhaustible.

Instead, fatherhood did something far less dramatic and far more confronting. It didn't ask me to hold up the world. It asked me to examine the parts of myself that couldn't.

I always wanted to be a father.

Not casually. Not someday-maybe. I wanted it the way some people want a dream job or a house with a wraparound porch. I grew up surrounded by women—three older sisters—and eventually became the proud uncle to four nieces and a nephew. I had logged hours. I had changed diapers. I had rocked babies. I had practice.

More importantly, I had a vision.

In that vision, I was the stand-out dad. The calm one. The capable one. The kind of father who instinctively knew what his child needed. I would be hands-on. Patient. Emotionally available. I would support my wife in heroic, cinematic ways—cooking elegant meals while she recovered, anticipating her needs before she spoke them, thriving in the chaos while other men quietly unraveled.

I wasn't just excited to become a dad.
I expected to be good at it.

So when the first three months knocked the wind out of me, I didn't just feel tired.
I felt betrayed by my own fantasy.

I felt jealous when my daughter quieted instantly in my wife's arms after I had tried the exact same hold for twenty minutes. I felt anger that didn't make sense and scared me when it showed up. I felt guilty for wanting a break from a baby who had only just arrived. I missed my old life in small, embarrassing ways—like the ability to sleep off exhaustion or surprise my wife with an elaborate dinner instead of handing her a reheated plate between feedings.
And underneath all of it was a question I didn't know how to say out loud:
What if I'm not actually built for this?
No one told me that fatherhood could feel like this.

Most parenting books prepare you for logistics—feeding schedules, sleep regressions, diaper brands, developmental milestones. They do not prepare you for the emotional whiplash of loving your child more than anything you've ever known while simultaneously feeling overwhelmed, irrationally frustrated, jealous, doubtful, and occasionally desperate for space.
They don't talk about the anger.
They don't talk about the jealousy.
They don't talk about the guilt that follows both.

And they definitely don't talk about how crushing it feels when the father you imagined doesn't match the one staring back at you in the nursery mirror at 3:17 a.m.
This book is not a guide to perfect parenting.
It's a confession.

It's the story of the first three months of my daughter's life—the hospital haze, the sleep deprivation fog, the identity crisis, the advice Olympics, the jealousy, the resentment, the small victories, and the moment I realized that none of those feelings meant I was failing.

If you are reading this while exhausted, irritated, confused, or quietly questioning yourself…
You are not broken.
You are not uniquely unqualified.
And you are not alone.

The first three months are not just about keeping a newborn alive.

They are about surviving the collapse of the fantasy and building something more honest in its place.

Let's start there.

Chapter 1

The Hospital Haze

In the movies and TV shows, you often see the triumphant husband holding his wife's hand as she heroically makes the final screaming push. A second later, the cries of a baby humble everyone in the room, and the parents are either asked to snip a cord or immediately handed an oddly immaculate-looking newborn for a victorious, tear-stained coddle.

My experience was more like a medical drama that skipped the commercial break. One moment I was snipping the umbilical, the next, Nora was laid in Kate's arms for the briefest moment before a nurse briskly rushed her to the infant bed for treatment. Nora had tried to take a breath too soon and inhaled fluid. There was no triumphant cry; just the terrifying, deafening sound of medical monitors and suction pulling fluid out of our baby's lungs. Waiting for that first breath felt like hours. When she finally cried—a small, perfect sound—the relief was so profound it felt like an emotional tsunami.

The joy of holding her, seeing her, and sharing that moment with my wife, Kate, felt almost disorienting in its intensity. There are no adequate words in any language to describe that incredible, transcendent high. In that moment, it felt exactly the way I had imagined it would. Powerful. Expansive. As if love itself had expanded my capacity overnight. If this was fatherhood, I was ready to carry anything.

But then you blink, and suddenly you're in the **recovery room**; just the three of you. And that profoundly deep joy drops off a cliff.
This is the **Euphoria Crash**.

All of your adrenaline plummets, your brain goes from "focused on survival" to "unplugged," and you find yourself asking, *what the hell are we supposed to do now?* Do I need to memorize all the pamphlets the nurse just gave me about baby poops? Do I start filling out the paperwork for a birth certificate and a social security number? What if I fill something out wrong and somehow my daughter never gets an SSN and can't open a bank account? It's remarkable how quickly the mind moves from wonder to responsibility. One minute you're staring at a miracle. The next, you're afraid you'll misfile a form and ruin her financial future.

For me, the husband and newly minted walking anxiety attack, I felt like I was juggling two life-and-death priorities. Nora needs to be prepped for her next feeding, diaper change, or nurse check. Kate just delivered a baby and I'm not sure she should even leave the bed! My inner monologue was screaming: **"Go help your wife, you idiot! I don't know what she needs right now but she needs something—she just pushed a baby out of her hooha!"**

And then, just when you might close your eyes for a precious forty minutes, an angel arrives. The hospital staff were absolute angels, but they were angels who had a strict policy of interrupting our sleep every forty minutes. Though they tried their best to avoid disturbing us, there was no ignoring the sweet, sweet wails of our daughter when she was gently prodded for yet another test.

It all merges into one thick, surreal **Hospital Haze**. I even remember a nurse kindly offering to take Nora to the nursery so Kate and I could get some sleep. In my delirious state, I instantly thought, *Why would I send her away? She literally just got here!* My wife and I eventually agreed, of course, because the nurse was a genius in scrubs trying to throw us a lifeline. But the sheer **idiocy** of my initial thought just goes to show how truly thick that haze can get.

The hospital is designed to keep you safe, which unfortunately means it also gives you a dangerous, **false sense of security** about your exhaustion level.

For the first forty-eight hours, you're running on pure, uncut adrenaline spikes, residual panic, and the endless stream of snacks and bad coffee from the hospital cafeteria. If you're wild, you might order the occasional delivery meal. Sure, the nurses are waking you every hour for a check, and the baby is demanding a meal, a clean diaper, or just a tiny scream-off, but it all feels… manageable. There is a building full of baby experts at your disposal. Someone else is stocking the diapers and cleaning the room. There's a button to press if you're scared. And you don't need to worry about work or meal planning tomorrow (yet). It's like being at a five-star, all-inclusive, hospital-themed resort where the staff occasionally hands you an adorable crying potato.

You tell yourself, "Look at us! We're crushing this! We only got 2.5 hours of sleep, but it was *high-quality* 2.5 hours! If this is 'hard,' we're totally fine." You genuinely believe you've found some internal reservoir of superhuman endurance. You *are* tired but not so tired that you consciously force every limb in your body to move.

This is the lie. This is the **Hospital Haze** at its most deceptive.

The hospital doesn't just support you. It buffers you. It absorbs the first wave of responsibility so gently that you can mistake adrenaline for competence. But adrenaline fades faster than responsibility does.

What you don't realize is that your job description is about to radically change from "part-time caretaker with paid support staff" to **"24/7, unpaid, uncertified, lone security guard for a highly combustible, tiny human."**

You're stacking up a debt of sleep you can't possibly repay, and the interest rate is compounding faster than you realize. But you won't know that until you finally get to the finish line, the car ride home.

That deceptive feeling of control is shattered the moment you realize you have to pack up the most precious, fragile cargo in human history and put it into a metal box traveling at high speeds.

For us, the chariot of choice was the Doona—the all-in-one car seat and stroller. I installed the base over a month prior and spent a meticulous afternoon practicing every button, knob, and strap until I could practically get that thing in the car with my eyes closed. Then, I didn't touch it for three weeks, because apparently, my brain assumed one day of training was enough to pass the *"Don't Kill Your Newborn on the Way Home"* certification exam.

The moment of truth arrives. I pull the car up to the hospital pickup lane, open the back seat and... wait, how do I detach the stroller? I *know* this. I did it twenty times... three weeks and several full nights of sleep ago. I finally figured it out after a few seconds, but then more panic resurfaces:

where is that button to release the wheels? All this head-scratching is happening while Kate is holding our daughter, patiently waiting in a wheelchair with the nurse, and I am pretending everything is totally normal.

When I finally get the stroller set up properly, the true pillar of fears collapses in: *I haven't checked the base straps in a while. Did they get looser after a few weeks? Is the chest clip on Nora high enough? Is it too high?*

Suddenly, every movement becomes exceptionally careful and precise. Folding the wheels back up must be done without shaking Nora. I'm attaching the stroller to the base—*OMG, I bumped the stroller against the car when I tried to set it in!* Nora is still breathing? Check! All this happens in a matter of minutes, and we haven't even left the parking spot.

When we finally strap ourselves in and leave the hospital pickup lane, a few things dawn on me at once:

1. **We are officially on our own; no more nurse button**
2. **Everything on the road is big and fast.**
3. **Danger. Is. Everywhere.**

I absolutely paused at every possible stop sign for a socially unacceptable amount of time. I drove exclusively in the right-hand lane on the highway, barely hovering at the speed limit because I was busy searching the horizon for phone-distracted drivers, large trucks hauling loose materials, and eighteen-wheelers with spiked lug nuts. My hands could not possibly grip the steering wheel any tighter. It was a sixteen-mile journey of white-knuckled terror, fueled by the sleep debt I'd been blissfully ignoring.

As I gripped the steering wheel, it felt like I was carrying the weight of the world. Not in some grand, heroic way — but in the most literal sense. My entire world was sitting in the back seat. Responsibility wasn't theoretical anymore. It was buckled into a car seat behind me. But as I took the final highway exit towards our neighborhood, a sweet thought wedged its way through all the terror and anxiety. In a few moments, we would show Nora her home—the room we had built for her over months of anticipation. Nora would finally get to see something she only got to hear about in utero; the first physical personification of our love for her.

The house looked exactly as we had left it, but it felt different the moment we walked through the door. Calmer. Warmer. Ours—plus one.

The hospital had been extraordinary. The nurses were attentive. The systems were reassuring. There was comfort in knowing someone else was quietly watching over the details. But there is a different kind of comfort in your own couch, your own kitchen, your own walls. The relief of being home settled in quickly, steady and grounding.

We were glad to be back.

Kate is a highly skilled nurse practitioner. I never doubted her ability to care for our daughter. If anything, I felt fortunate to have her knowledge and composure in moments that might have rattled someone else. But I didn't want our home to feel like another shift for her. I didn't want her expertise to be the thing that steadied us. I wanted to be competent enough that she could just be Mom.

That realization sharpened something in me.

This wasn't about whether we were capable. We were. It was about ownership. There was no one else responsible now. No escalation. No second layer. Whatever came next would belong to us.

As I stood in the nursery doorway and looked at the room we had built for her, I felt the magnitude of it settle in—not as spectacle, not as heroism, but as responsibility. Our entire world was asleep down the hall.

We were home.

And now it was ours to carry.

Chapter 2

The Fog of Sleep Deprivation

The In-Home Zombie Reality

Being home initially came with a thin blanket of comfort that eased some of the newborn-induced anxiety. This was our space, our safe space, and we knew where to find everything. Crucially, though, it was also the space we had to clean ourselves, and the space our little Nora would soon take logistical ownership of.

Maybe it was the comfort of the familiar couch, or maybe we had finally reached the limit of our sleep debt, but the sheer exhaustion was beginning to take its toll. The clock stopped being useful almost immediately. Time was no longer measured in hours but in cycles—feeding, burping, changing, swaddling, and the fragile hope of sleep. Nora's forty-five-minute cycles could feel like an hour while also disappearing in an instant. We were no longer governed by any traditional clock. The sun and moon had no say in our rest. Our bedtime was whenever Nora slept, and there was no need to clean something that wasn't strictly necessary.

At first, the exhaustion was almost funny. I caught myself laughing at how dramatically my brain slowed down. Simple tasks required the kind of concentration usually reserved for assembling furniture or doing long division. I started narrating my own mistakes out loud just to stay entertained.

By forty-eight hours post-discharge, the hospital coffee and cafeteria suddenly seemed like a fair exchange for the post-partum nursery lifeline. I almost missed the nurses and doctors interrupting our twilight sleep to check the monitors and our status. After seventy-two hours, when you realize you haven't changed clothes since your first shower at home, you start to feel like the exhaustion is **terminal**.

Simple tasks that I used to complete with sheer muscle memory became a conscious struggle. Making a peanut butter and jelly sandwich? I forgot the jelly. It's too late for the jelly. There is only energy for a peanut butter sandwich, now. Sacrifices must be made. There is no escape from **zombification**. It wasn't alarming. It was just… slower. Like my brain had quietly switched from autopilot to manual transmission.

This led to a strange and paradoxical cycle:

1. **Awake:** When Nora was awake, I wanted to hold and soothe her, showering her with songs and love.
2. **The Nudge:** Then the sleep deprivation would nudge me, and I'd be counting down the seconds to her next sleep cycle. It could not come soon enough.
3. **The Circus:** Nora is finally asleep after a circus of rocking, bouncing, and what I can only describe as rhythmic walking.
4. **The Rest:** We'd clean only what was necessary (nipple shields, burp rags, maybe a load of hospital laundry) and finally rest our weary bodies.
5. **The Command:** Just as we drifted off to sleep, we hear Nora's fuss; commanding our bodies to prepare for the next cycle.

Starting back at the 'Awake' stage of the cycle was certainly the most tiring and uplifting part of the cycle. Yes, she's awake before you are rested but she might also give you her first smile or wrap her tiny hand around your whole finger. Almost to signal and remind me that we are her whole world and she is ours. The moments and memories built here helped propel me through the remaining stages but there is still mounting exhaustion that exacerbates my emotions. The strange thing was that I still felt capable. The fatigue was obvious, but it felt manageable—as long as I stayed focused. As long as I kept moving.

Lectures to Inanimate Objects

After enough cycles, I found myself experiencing surges of **totally irrational frustration** that would rival some cartoon characters. Some loose diapers would fall out of the bin while I was pulling one out to change Nora's soiled diaper, and suddenly, I was having an entire lecture playing out in my head. *"Really, guys? You had to jump out of your home? Because I don't have more important things to do than to put you back in your bin?"*

Very suddenly, I was having intense internal dialogues with inanimate objects and the universe at large. *"Dear universe, please let Nora sleep just a little longer. I promise to be better at recycling."*

The universe did not oblige.

You might be asking, *"Didn't you and Kate take shifts so one of you could get a little more sleep per shift?"* An idea which sounds clever, but crumbles under the barrage of short sleep/wake windows and breastfeeding. There was little rest for Kate, and I needed to be alert enough to be her extra hands. I needed to clean and dry breastfeeding accessories like nipple shields, help change Nora's clothes if there was an accident, switch out burp rags if one got too much 'burp,' and the possibilities go on. As the partner who did not need to recover from growing, birthing, and feeding a newborn, I needed to take care of the hour-to-hour needs of my family.

This inevitably became our fog of sleep deprivation – thick enough to slow everything down, but not yet heavy enough to make me doubt that I could push through it.

Chapter 3

The Identity Crisis – Losing My Mind and My Roles

The exhaustion of the previous chapter does more than make you sleepy; it strips away your ability to be the person you thought you were. It starts with a painful, nagging realization: **I am failing at the job I trained for, the job I thought I was built for, and, most importantly, the job my daughter needed the most.**

The Myth of the Problem-Solving Parent

The problem wasn't that things were going wrong. The problem was that I thought I should already know how to make them go right. Before Nora arrived, I honestly believed I would be the **calm, practical, problem-solving dad**. I read the books. I took in all the advice. I was prepared for the logistics. Between Kate and myself, we even had ten nieces and nephews; how could I possibly get more prepared? I was not prepared for the existential dread that sets in when you realize your best efforts are constantly falling short of your own standards. Every day, I felt like I was just getting a little worse.

Preparation had always worked for me before. Read the instructions, follow the steps, solve the problem. I assumed fatherhood would follow a similar flow with minor improvising.

In my pre-parent life, I was great at planning for direct cause and effect. If I worked hard, I got results. If I read the assembly instructions, I could build the shelf (Ikea instructions, included). I had the focus and foresight to plan for weeks and months in advance. I knew just how to prepare Kate's latte, when the house was due for another vacuuming, and seldom missed a single ingredient on the grocery list. Parenting, however, is a game with rules that change every hour without notice, and a tiny, adorable referee who communicates exclusively through **ear-splitting screams**.

I'd try to figure out why Nora was crying. I'd run through the checklist:

1. Diaper? Clean.
2. Hungry? Fed thirty minutes ago.
3. Too hot? Too cold?
4. The swaddle? I'd spend fifteen minutes meticulously wrapping her like a perfect, tight burrito, only for her to Houdini her way out in sixty seconds, looking at me like, *"Rookie mistake, Dad."*

I even went so far as to buy special, easy **Velcro swaddles**, and this worked for a time—until our magician pulled another fast one on me in the middle of the night. I would rest with my smug satisfaction until I heard a faint sucking sound at 3 a.m. and turn to see a single free arm—Nora's late-night snack.

At bath time, I would try to prepare everything so Kate could just bring Nora into the bathtub without additional work. After all, she was getting as little sleep as me or less, and her body was also physically working to produce food; she needed as little additional complication as possible. But as soon as Nora was in the tub, Kate would give me a quizzical look because I forgot the washcloth, or the soap, or the towel, or I grabbed a onesie that was too big or too small.

None of these moments were catastrophic. They were small, forgettable mistakes. But they stacked on top of each other quietly, each one chipping away at the version of myself I thought would show up in this role. The hardest part of early fatherhood wasn't the baby. It was confronting the gap between the father I imagined and the father I actually was.

It's a constant, low-grade sense of failure. You're supposed to be this child's protector, translator, and master comforter—or at least **one of the**

comforters. Yet you can't decode the difference between a hunger cry, a gas cry, and an "I'm just mad at the universe" cry. I would look at my exhausted wife and feel this white-hot stab of panic, thinking, *How are we going to keep this child alive if I can't even figure out why she is screaming every moment she's awake?* Every time I fumbled a bottle or struggled to soothe her, I felt the gap widening between the **competent man I thought I was** and the frantic, unqualified person rocking awkwardly in the bedroom.

I would transition constantly between the rocking chair, the exercise ball, and rhythmic walking, praying to whatever deity was listening that some *Mortal Kombat*-like combo would bring her to sleep. This is often the place where Nora's cries and my own feelings of failure would echo and reinforce each other.

The Slow Realization of the Partner Failure

It takes time for your brain to process the secondary damage, because your focus is entirely on the tiny dictator. But once the initial survival panic settles into a daily grind, you start to see the collateral damage in your relationship.

The exhaustion is a shield, but it can also make you a **terrible spouse**. I tried to support Kate, I wanted to be her rock, but my emotional tank was running on fumes. I looked at her and felt both immense, protective love for the mother of our child and a strange, quiet grief for the loss of my wife. She was just as tired as me (if not more), but she seemed to move through the chaos with a steadiness I couldn't replicate. It made me aware of the gap between how I imagined I would handle this and how I actually was.

Our previous dynamic—the easy conversation, the shared jokes, the spontaneous connection—is barely there. Interactions start to feel transactional: *"Did you clean the breast pump parts?" "Have you eaten yet?" "Is the sound machine on the white noise setting?"*

This is the part no one truly warns you about: the **silent resentment** that builds. You're both so tired and so sure you're doing more than the other that stupid, minuscule things become flashpoints. The tone used to ask about a burp rag, the fact that a dirty plate made it from the coffee table to the counter but not the sink—these tiny missteps in the partnership become part of a growing mound of resentment and annoyance. You realize you're not annoyed about burp rags; you're annoyed about the fact that you're both too exhausted to be **kind**.

The Non-Existent "New Normal"

Going into parenthood, everyone knows and expects their lives to change, but the degree of shift is unimaginable. It was one thing to hear about it or watch my siblings go through it, but being entrenched first-hand? The experience is too intense to adequately describe.

In the months leading up to Nora's birth, I told myself to expect exhaustion, changes in our home dynamic, and to prepare to build a new **'normal'** for our families day-to-day. The fallacy here is that there *is* no 'normal'. There is no steady state in these first few months because once you build an ounce of routine or find an hourly solution to the latest reason for newborn fuss, the reason changes. Everything feels like it starts over, and you're left to play **sleep-deprived detective** all over again.

For example, Nora was always feeding or screaming when she was awake. We knew it couldn't be colic—she was too young, and besides, colic is a diagnosis of exclusion. A few weeks later, we figured it was **silent reflux**. Nora was likely spitting up enough during feeds to burn her throat but not enough to expel onto a burp rag or lose weight. The medicine helped at first, and we started to get a little more peace. We naturally began to build a routine around this newfound nugget of peace, but then she had trouble sleeping again a few days later. Did we need something stronger? Was she going through another sleep regression? Was it a misdiagnosis? There was no way to definitively know without invasive testing, and our sweet girl was too young for that.

Kate even tested the possibility of a breast milk allergy exacerbating the silent reflux, so we went on a long **diet elimination journey**. Removing dairy, eggs, nuts, etc., until Kate was practically eating steamed veggies. After each elimination, we thought we were seeing progress, and so the hopeful cycle to normalize our routines would start, then abruptly stop again when Nora had trouble calming to sleep.

It was a **vicious cycle**. We'd think we found a solution and integrate it into our daily routine, then it would stop working, and we'd have to start from ground zero again. Sometimes, there was no solution needed; Nora was just changing her natural sleep and wake windows. All we could do was keep trying to adapt to this wild ride. It was like getting in a sports car and hitting the open road, except the open road had **booby-traps** that would launch unprovoked stop signs at you. Eventually you learn to brace yourself but there is no getting around the jostling.

Chapter 4

The Advice Olympics

Before Nora was even born, we were inundated with advice from all corners of life. From close family and friends to neighbors, co-workers, and newfound acquaintances in line at the self-checkout. Everything seemed important. It felt like I was studying for a college final exam, except the exam was going to last decades and the study material was infinite. Kate and I had our own stack of books about infant care and an additional book or two gifted from friends. Just like that college exam, when the big day arrived, we felt like we were going to be as ready as we would ever be.

The sad truth is, most everything I read to prepare was virtually wiped from my mind and replaced by the **fog of sleep deprivation**. I could barely think clearly; I was just desperate for working solutions amid Nora's regular screams.

Friends and family contacted us to make sure we were still functional humans, asking the inevitable, *"How are you? How's the baby sleeping? Are you guys getting any rest?"* I always said things were fine at first, but eventually I was too exhausted for automated social niceties, and the candor just **vomited out of me**.

The response? Naturally, everyone wants to help! *"Have you tried A, B, C? This used to work for us!"* or *"I read somewhere..."* or *"One of my friends tried..."*

This was all coming from a heartfelt and well-rested place, but if I had to hear one more person suggest **elevating the crib**, **use an exercise ball** to gently bounce, or maybe Nora's just **gassy**, I was going to put my head through a wall. Specifically, drywall, because there was not enough energy for brick. Advice sounds comforting, in theory. In practice, it mostly reminded me how many things we had already tried.

The Fast-Forward Frustration

The most maddening advice came from those closest to me—and ironically, those who seemed to understand the least about my current state of mind.

I have a text group with my three older sisters, all of whom have older children. I would text them in my delirium when I needed more brain power to resolve an issue with Nora. Everyone was on deck! Firing off solutions and suggestions at 7 p.m.! I wanted so badly to feel grateful in that moment for the prompt responses, but all I could focus on was the fact that every suggestion was something I had already tried and was **failed**.

I literally wanted to put the conversation on fast-forward and zoom past the first five to ten suggestions. I needed creative ideas to help soothe my daughter, not the same thing everyone says. *Of course,* I already tried those things, because **EVERYONE SAYS THEM!**

For the record, some things everyone usually said —which never worked for us—were: look for sleep cues, keep her up longer so she'll fall asleep faster, and the literal opposite: take her for a nap earlier because maybe she's overtired. Nora managed to dodge the effects of all these commonplace musings with the grace of a Russian ballerina. Nora was truly focused on being one of a kind and mom and dad were paying the price.

The Toxic Relationship with Dr. Google

Predictably, I turned to **Dr. Google** for some answers. This instantly became my most toxic relationship. It's so easy to pull out your phone and search for every abnormal behavior and symptom your infant exhibits, and that is precisely the first piece of real advice anyone should give you: do this as little as possible.

Why? Two reasons:

1. **Every anxiety-inducing response you can imagine exists on the internet.**
2. **If/When you inevitably look at social media, you will feel like an even worse parent.**

Am I aware that people only post happy-go-lucky content with their kids? Of course! Would people randomly post themselves sitting on a couch, styling a three-day-old, spit-up-covered sweater while sporting the latest burp rag accessory beside their newborn? Probably not. But does that awareness matter to my visceral emotions when I scroll past videos of dads effortlessly crushing it at fatherhood? Also, probably not.

I found myself tumbling down Reddit rabbit holes with responses ranging from, **"totally normal for us and lasted 2 years,"** to the most useless and enraging response on the internet: **"just a sleep regression."** If you search anything related to your baby's weekly age and sleep, a post about a regression at that exact age will appear. Was the occasional soul-crushing sleep regression, correct? Yes, but even a squirrel who digs enough holes will eventually find a nut.

I will attest to eventually digging out the occasional helpful hint, but I seldom found a direct, working answer. The initial idea of silent **reflux** causing Nora discomfort—and thus taking two hours to rock her to sleep—came from the internet. It was something the pediatrician entertained but wasn't the final answer. Fast-forward several more weeks, and the reflux rabbit hole led us to possible allergens in Kate's breast milk, which ultimately led us to an entirely different pediatrician who finally turned us onto a specific baby formula (the final answer-ish). Clearly the internet didn't give us the answer, but did it lead us there? Kinda?

These tiny crises are just the tip of the iceberg. Advice for parents really does feel like the **Olympics**, at times. There are categories of events: Medical, Nutrition, Equipment, Sleep, Clothes, Bathing, Breastfeeding (a little more for Kate than me), and so on. As parents, we can't "win" in all these events all the time, but we never want to stop trying.

Chapter 5

The Partner Paradox

The Co-Worker Marriage

The shift from a couple with an active social life to two sleep-deprived caretakers operating a tiny, volatile human was immediate and profound. We weren't having knock-down, drag-out arguments, which felt like a win, but we were a touch snippy. The exhaustion stripped away all the padding of polite social niceties. Instead of fights, we had **moods**—and the most frequent mood was one of quiet, aimless annoyance. I would catch myself staring blankly into space, my brain buffering, and Kate would immediately get annoyed, which annoyed me. It was a spectacular, negative self-reinforcing cycle.

Our relationship became less of a partnership and more of a **logistics team** running a two-person baby startup with impossible hours. The most romantic thing we did was silently clean the kitchen. There were no discussions or affectionate gestures of appreciation; it was purely mechanical. While cleaning nipple shields, breast pump parts, and general dishes, I felt like an assembly worker just doing what had to be done to get to the next "thing"—which was usually another feeding or the futile pursuit of an hour of sleep. The entire operation was defined by transactional language: *"She woke up at 3:15," "The diaper pail is full,"* or the ever-romantic, *"Where did you put the nipple shields?"*

The constant grind made us lose all sense of time; each wake window simply bled into the next, and time seemed to slow down. **Leaving the house for even a simple errand felt like planning a military operation.** The sheer logistics were overwhelming—God forbid we forget a single critical item and have to rush home anyway. We had the occasional visitor but most left us to our own devices, unaware of when we would be busy or trying to rest so erring on the side of caution. It felt like being on a **deserted island** with my best friend. A little less sun and sand, perhaps, but it was just Kate, Nora, and myself, trying to survive day to day.

We had become the world's most stressed-out roommates, united only by the screaming baby in the next room and a desperate desire for the other person to handle the next problem. We were a well-oiled machine, but the oil was optimism and the fuel was fear.

The Paradox

Yet, in the middle of all the mechanical madness, the paradox held true. The moment we finally got to share after all the chaos was more powerful than any date night or romantic gesture we'd had before.

When Nora finally fell asleep at night after a feeding, and we successfully executed the delicate, **slow-motion escape** from the room—like two spies trying to disarm a bomb without setting off the pressure plate—there was a deep calm and connection. The culmination of all the chaos, the irrational frustration, and the mutual tension would suddenly evaporate. We had earned that daily moment of peace for each other. Standing in the hallway, sharing a whispered summary of the night's battle, we'd exchange a look that said: *We are so tired, we are so annoyed, but we did this. We survived this shift.* That moment of shared, silent victory was the proof that the original **"us"** was still intact, just currently buried under a mountain of burp cloths and sleep debt.

Chapter 6

Mom, Dad, and the Kingdom of Cryptic Cries

During these first 3 months, after Nora had arrived home, she was often either crying, eating, or sleeping. There were shockingly rare moments of calm. We felt like we were bamboozled by everyone's comments of, "the first few months are kind of boring! The baby just eats, sleeps, and poops a lot." What we wouldn't give for that to be the case! There is a natural evolution of methodologies when it comes to trying to soothe your baby out of their crying. Ours went a bit as follows:

1. **Level 1:** Just keep trying to test the usual suspects! Hunger, sleep, and diaper change!
2. **Level 2:** A more methodical Level 1 with overlapping feeding and sleeping plus elaborate tactics to try to make Nora extra sleepy for longer naps. (Be warned, this did NOT work. Keeping your baby up later in hopes they will sleep longer will only make them harder to put to sleep and so much crankier in the process)
3. **Level 3 (Enter the Internet):** Attempt to decode the literal crying sounds because all babies are auto-magically born with a universal cry-lingo… or so the many blogs and videos would lead you to believe

4. **Level 4:** Paying for a book, professional sleep consultant, or online "parenting tutor" to learn about sleep and wake cycles for each week of your baby's life and hope you catch the proper sleepy queues
5. **Level 5:** You promise to give your newborn a pony and hope they bless you with a prolonged respite

When we entered "Level 3," Kate and I were meticulously trying to recreate what we expected the cries for hunger, sleep, and discomfort to sound like. All we had to start with was text describing the sounds, so we had to fill in the literal sounds between the two of us. With absolutely no context, if you walked into the room, you would unquestionably have assumed we lost our minds. "I think the sleepy cry is something like an 'oohwa' and maybe the hunger sound has more bass? Something like a 'neh.'" Lets be honest, while reading that last sentence, you totally tried to make those sounds and I hope you sounded better than us. For a time, we were sure we were getting the hang of decoding cries, but the seeming success was short-lived. Were we on an episode of MythBusters, I would label baby cry decoding, busted.

Before moving on to "Level 4," we tried sound machines with white noise, blue noise, and every other color of the rainbow hoping to find a pot of restful gold. I even transitioned between walking, bouncing on an exercise ball, and performing something called a Tai Chi Walk. Surprisingly unremarkable results. Sometimes, Nora would calm just from me returning her to Kate. The narrative was that newborns could smell their mothers unique scent and had an instinctive preference. I have no idea how much truth is in that narrative but who was I to question if that plan occasionally worked. Though, as a father and spouse, having to give your baby over (even if it is to your husband/wife) for them to calm down can make you feel disappointed in yourself.

On one hand, I would question why I couldn't figure out how to soothe Nora as her father. On the other hand, I *needed* to find a way to soothe her so Kate could have a break. I didn't have the biology to feed my child, so I needed to find another significant way to contribute in these moments. Failure to do this one thing was sometimes emotionally crushing. "Why isn't anything I am doing working? I literally had one job!" I felt like a walking failure meme. My wife is exhausted, my child is fussing, and after my useless attempts all that came of it was my handing my fussing child back to my exhausted wife. Way to go, super dad.

The Last Hope: Paying for a Solution (Level 4)

After free advice from the internet failed, we reached **Level 4**. Basically, throw money at the problem. This is a special kind of desperation, where you literally exchange money for the *hope* of uninterrupted hours of sleep.

We bought the sleep-training books, joined the special subscription sites, and considered selling a kidney for a consultation with a certified sleep expert. Our biggest leap of faith was buying the **exorbitantly expensive SNOO bassinet**. We simply could not sustain bouncing and rocking Nora for two hours for virtually every single nap, and the SNOO promised a robotic, tireless replacement. You are literally paying for a machine to do what your body can no longer physically manage.

It was the feeling that, perhaps, the solution wasn't common sense, but a guarded industry secret only available to those willing to invest. We became data scientists of our own child, tracking every nap, input, and output, all in search of a pattern that simply doesn't exist yet. And inevitably, even this highly paid, meticulously tracked effort yielded... another dead end. We did find one subscription that yielded some helpful hints, but the advice was broken down into age groupings. If you wanted to continue getting help after a certain age group, you had to pay another fee. You look at that renewal notice and just feel your **bank account drain like your sanity**.

Like any good parent, we inevitably reached **Level 5: Unrealistic Bribery**. We absolutely offered to buy her a pony… someday. Maybe Nora is more of a purse and shoes kind of gal? How about an Hermes Birkin bag with some Valentino shoes! Level 5 isn't a true promise of delivery but more of a, "I need to laugh or I'll cry," type of situation. For a time, you will find yourself bouncing back and forth between Level's 4 and 5 because no matter how difficult the situation gets, your baby is still your sweet treasure.

The Grand Finale: The 72-Hour Miracle

To give you the full picture of the "Crying Mystery," I need to fast-forward past the repetitive cycles of Level 4 and Level 5, straight to the end of our fourth trimester. After three months of playing sleep-deprived detective, we finally caught a break, and it didn't come from a book or a $1,600 bassinet. It came from family.

We contacted my cousin, a pediatrician who happened to share our exact family demographic: Asian male, Caucasian female, and a young daughter of his own. We laid out the evidence—the screams, the hours of rocking, the elusive sleep. He listened and promptly cut through the noise with a single recommendation: **Hypoallergenic formula.**

He suspected Nora had an allergy to something in Kate's breast milk. He explained that there's no quick, easy test for specific allergens, and an elimination diet—while valiant—could take weeks of Kate eating nothing but steamed air and hope, with no guarantee of a result. He gave us two formula recommendations and a chillingly specific timeline: *"You'll know if it works within 24 to 72 hours based on how she sleeps."*

That was all the motivation we needed. We raced to the grocery store like we were in the final lap of the Indy 500, grabbed samples of both formulas, and prepped the first bottle for the bedtime feeding.

That night, for the first time in her life, Nora slept through the entire night.

When Kate and I woke up the next morning and saw the sun, we didn't feel rested—we felt **pure, unadulterated terror**. We sat up in a panic, convinced that something was horribly wrong or that our bodies had finally experienced a brain-initiated, self-induced preservation coma that rendered us deaf to her cries. We scrambled to the baby monitor like it was a crime scene.

Reviewing the footage confirmed the impossible: we hadn't neglected her; she had just found relief. She was still, peaceful, and—most importantly—quiet.

In that moment, we felt a profound, heavy mix of emotions. There was the sheer joy of finally finding a solution, but it was shadowed by a deep sense of **parental guilt**. We realized our sweet girl had spent the first three months of her existence in a state of prolonged discomfort. Aside from the crying and some later skin reddening, she never had "typical" allergy symptoms. Our first pediatrician's best guess was silent reflux—where stomach acid splashes into the throat—and while the meds helped a little, they were never the "answer."

Once we switched to the hypoallergenic formula, the "reflux" vanished, the medication went into the trash, and our lives were changed forever. It also planted a quiet realization: sometimes the solution isn't hidden in the advice you already have—it's waiting somewhere just outside your circle.

Chapter 7

Finding Your Tribe (Or Not)

The Proximity Problem

In those first few months, the idea of a "Parent Group" felt like a myth. We didn't have a "dating scene" for new friends because we were too exhausted to even look. Besides, where would you even start to look for newborn parents near you? The labor and delivery post-partum hospital database? I could be wrong, but I think HIPAA regulations would frown upon that for some reason. We were stuck in a catch-22 of isolation: we desperately needed to connect with people in the same season of life, but the logistics of packing up the entire house just to go *somewhere* to meet them seemed impossible.

We had two main hurdles that no one really prepares you for:

1. **How do you find parent friends who are in the exact same newborn season?**
2. **How do you find them close enough that a 15-minute meltdown doesn't ruin the entire outing?**

For a long time, we had no answer. We had friends with newborns, but their distance made consistent connection a fantasy. We were a trio on an island, waiting for a flare gun that we would be too tired to fire.

The Grocery Store Confessional

When you're that isolated, your social filter doesn't just thin—it evaporates. I became a "desperate connector" in the most unlikely of places: the grocery store.

The "connection" happened at the locked baby formula cabinet. A kind woman came to unlock the door for me, and what should have been a simple "thank you" turned into a twenty-second, incoherent manifesto. The floodgates opened. I started rambling about the miracle of hypoallergenic formula, how it changed our lives, why it was so expensive, and how Nora was *finally* sleeping after three months of mystery. I was essentially a captive audience of one and thank goodness she was patient enough to let me finish my "TED Talk" before letting me go.

It later happened again at the self-checkout of a different grocery store. The attendant asked how old Nora was when she saw the formula, and once again, I unloaded the entire saga of our lives in the time it took to scan my remaining groceries. Interestingly, that same woman would catch Nora and I months later in the same aisle, greeting us with the kind of knowing smile you give a survivor.

The Quiet Shift of Seasons

While I was oversharing with grocery store employees, our existing social life was undergoing a quiet, drama-free shift. There was no big fallout or blow-up; it was just the reality of incompatible seasons.

After declining a series of party invites, dinner dates, and "just grab a drink" texts, the silence grew. We realized that for now, our lives were on a different frequency than many of our friends. We were prioritizing survival and family, and thankfully, our friends understood. Most of them had older kids or had seen this movie before, so there was no resentment—just a quiet, unspoken support and a mutual agreement that we'd meet again at a more "flexible" point in our lives.

Our little island was enough for us but it didn't mean we still didn't want more connection outside. I learned both could be true. Your spouse and child can be enough for you and you can still want outside connection. These types of connection are not mutually exclusive but seem paradoxical. Why do I want outside connection when my family is enough? For me, because they enrich each other in ways that are impossible without both.

Dads, Grilling, and the Search for Topic #2

When I finally encountered a "Dad Tribe" in our neighborhood, it was a fascinating exercise in social re-learning.

The initial connection is easy: you talk about the baby, the sleep (or lack thereof), and the gear. Bouncers, strollers, and sound machines – oh my! But once you exhaust the "Newborn Parent" talking points, there's a terrifying moment of: *What do we talk about now?* I could barely remember how to be a person, let alone a "guy's guy." I'm not into sports, so I didn't have that universal "man-lingo" to fall back on.

Thankfully, the neighborhood dads and I found our common ground through the holy trinity of fatherhood: **the grill, the whiskey, and the shared "thousand-yard stare."** We didn't need to talk about the game; we just needed to stand near a fire (or a blackstone), hold a glass, and acknowledge that we were all in the trenches together. Besides, once you reach your third glass of whiskey, the topic of conversation doesn't really matter.

The Neighborhood Collision

Our true "people" weren't found in a class, an app, or playplace—they were found by accident. Because Nora started walking early, she literally ran into our tribe. She'd bolt down the sidewalk at 10 months old and encounter a sweet little girl named Leti and her parents on our block, forcing us into the very social interactions we were too tired to seek out.

Those chance encounters introduced us to a whole web of newborn parents right on our street. We finally found the answer to our proximity problem. We didn't have to pack the car; we just had to open the front door and let Nora lead the way.

Chapter 8

The Small Victories

For the first three months, my definition of a "win" was purely defensive. If the baby was breathing, the house wasn't on fire, and I hadn't accidentally put the remote in the refrigerator, I called it a successful day. I was playing a game where the best outcome was simply "not losing."

But after the formula miracle, something shifted. It wasn't just that Nora was sleeping; it was that **I was finally waking up.** The brain fog that had settled over me in the hospital haze began to thin, and for the first time, I felt the return of my own agency. I stopped feeling like a clumsy intern and started feeling like a specialist. This following is about that shift—the era of the "Small Victory," where I stopped surviving the chaos and started mastering it.

The Solo Win

The first real test of this new competence usually happens when you're "flying solo." Without Kate there to provide a second opinion or a second pair of hands, I was the final line of defense. For me, that moment happened in a random, empty parking lot.

Nora and I were in the car, and one moment she was comfy-cozy, and the next, she was suddenly and exceptionally upset. The cause became evident a few seconds later when the scent of a **grade-A blowout** reached the front seat. I pulled over immediately. Did I need an empty lot? No, but my brain instinctively calculated the "aromatic blast radius" of the situation and decided it was better to be safe than to annoy the general public.

As soon as I unstrapped her, I saw it: the textbook definition of a blowout. The contents of her diaper had reached her upper back, oozed out the sides, and made contact with the car seat. Old me would have crumbled. I would have entered a self-loathing internal monologue of "why me!?" I converted the trunk into a **surgical changing station**. I moved with calculated efficiency, deploying an abundance of wipes, a fresh change of clothes, and a specialized bag to contain the offending diaper. Just as soon as it started, it was over. We were back on the road. I was so proud of myself that I called Kate the second I got back in the driver's seat. I'd like to point out the immense restraint I employed by *not* texting her a picture of the damage; I felt the scale of my accomplishment was enough without the visual evidence.

Graduating to the Pro Leagues

That parking lot victory wasn't a fluke; it was a symptom of a larger change. About two weeks after the formula switch, I realized I was finally operating on **muscle memory**. I had officially graduated from the "Sleep-Deprived Detective" phase to the "Pro Father Leagues."

I stopped looking at the books and started looking at Nora. Depending on the pitch of the cry and the time of day, I just gravitated toward what she needed. The living room baby swing? A bottle? Her favorite toy? A diaper? I was all about instinctively predicting my baby girls' needs! I did not keep a tally for proper statistical analysis, but it felt like I was hitting an **80% accuracy rate**. In the world of newborn parenting, an 80%+ hit rate makes you an MVP. The "Identity Crisis" was beginning to fade, replaced by the quiet confidence of a father who was getting to know his daughter.

The Midnight Pit Stop

This new-found confidence allowed me to turn even the most grueling tasks into a point of pride. For example, once Nora established a nighttime sleep pattern, she would still occasionally wake up once for a feed. Instead of dreading it, I turned it into a logistical challenge.

I developed a routine so efficient it kept Nora from reaching a full wakeful state. My goal was simple: get the milk in and the diaper changed before her brain realized she was awake. Every night, I pre-staged the battlefield. One bottle was cleaned and pre-assembled; the measuring cup was staged; all diaper products were strategically placed to **minimize latency**.

As soon as I heard the first stirring on the monitor, I was up, initiating the plan. The process was so clean that pro race car pit stop designers would have been proud. By keeping her in that "sleepy haze," she would finish the last drop of milk and immediately drift back to sleep. Executing that routine felt like winning a championship every single night—a small, silent victory that proved we finally had this under control. The entire "midnight pit stop" took so little time, it hardly made a dent in my overall sleep; a mere interruptive drop in the ocean of my sleep.

Chapter 9

The Emotional Rollercoaster – When Love and Rage Share the Same Room

There were moments when the anger didn't arrive loudly.

It arrived slowly and with weight.

My heart would begin to beat heavier, each pump felt deliberate and amplified, like I could hear it echoing in my own ears. Not fast. Not frantic. Just slower and harder. Labored. A pressure would build behind my eyes—not quite pain, but something close to dizziness. My fingertips would start to tingle, as if my body were quietly bracing for impact.

At first, I tried to think my way out of it.

But constructive thought would evaporate quickly. The checklist that usually governed my responses—diaper, hunger, temperature, swaddle—would dissolve into noise. My mind, normally organized and solution-oriented, turned into a kind of internal rage room. Every frustration ricocheted off the walls and returned sharper. Out of all this mental chaos, my anger evolved into fear.

I was never afraid I would hurt Nora.

What frightened me was something subtler and more corrosive: what did it mean that I felt this way?

The anger itself wasn't the crisis. The crisis was unsustainability.

Not the crying. Not the sleep. Not the reflux. Unsustainability. The quiet realization that if this was the new normal, I didn't know how long I could hold myself together.

And that is what breaks capable men—not difficulty, but the belief that the difficulty may never end.

The episodes usually followed the same script.

Nora would be crying—full-bodied, red-faced, inconsolable. I would bounce, rock, swaddle, re-swaddle, check the diaper, check the bottle, adjust the thermostat, analyze wake windows. I approached it like a malfunctioning system I could debug if I just stayed methodical enough.

Nothing would change and I was left feeling helpless.

Helplessness is a unique kind of trigger for someone who prides himself on problem-solving. It erodes identity in real time. When effort produces no result, something deeper begins to shake.

And then Kate would take her.

Same room. Same temperature. Same techniques. Silence.

Relief would come first. Gratitude. A wave of love for both of them.

And then, quietly, something else.

Jealousy.

I wasn't jealous of my wife. I was jealous of instinct. Of biology. Of the unspoken bond that allowed her to quiet our daughter without negotiation.

I was jealous of certainty.

And then came shame for feeling jealous at all.

What kind of father feels displaced by his own child's comfort in her mother's arms?

No one tells you that biology can feel like rejection when you are exhausted enough.

The advice says: when you feel overwhelmed, set the baby down in a safe place and walk away.

So sometimes I did.

I would lay Nora in her crib and step into another room, trying to regulate my breathing. But distance didn't dissolve the tension. Even if her cries were muffled, I knew they were happening. That knowledge alone kept my nervous system on high alert.

The pounding didn't ease. The tingling didn't fade.

Instead, something heavier settled in.

Shame.

I had spiraled so far away from problem-solving that I couldn't think about anything except how unsustainable I felt. The question stopped being, "How do I fix this?" and became, "How long can I survive this?"

A week?

Two weeks?

Two months?

The not knowing hollowed me out. At least exhaustion has a predictable cause and effect. Uncertainty stretches infinitely.

Nora didn't ask for whatever was causing her discomfort. She had no language for it. No understanding of why her body felt wrong or why sleep wouldn't come.

I was the adult in the room.

I was supposed to cope.

This was my duty and the manifestation of my love.

What did it say about me when I couldn't do it?

The anger that overwhelmed me and left me ashamed was never about her. It was about the collapse of the image I had built of myself.

Before she was born, I believed I would be calm under pressure. Experienced. Naturally equipped. I had logged hours as an uncle. I had changed diapers and soothed nieces. I thought I had earned some invisible badge of readiness.

Instead, I found myself questioning whether fatherhood had been a fantasy I wasn't qualified to inhabit.

That's the part no one talks about.

The way doubt doesn't just whisper—it indicts.

I tried to compartmentalize.

I told myself this was temporary. That I could shelve the frustration and revisit it later. But how do you compartmentalize something with no known ending? How do you put a time limit on a situation that has none?

The strategy collapsed under the weight of time.

I avoided leaning on Kate. She was recovering from childbirth. She was sustaining Nora with her own body. She was navigating the same stress and exhaustion I was, and somehow still managing to calm our daughter more effectively than I could. Asking her to carry my emotional weight on top of that felt preposterous.

So I carried it alone.

I had family I reached out to occasionally. I had a friend with a son born just days after Nora. I wanted someone who understood.

But their son was sleeping well—for a newborn. Feeding well. Described as "the kind of baby that makes you want to have a second." My family was always attentive but their experiences were still so different, they didn't fully grasp my struggle.

I felt heard but not seen.

No one knew how to help me. Not even me.

And when you don't know how to help yourself, isolation feels logical.

There was a line from my wedding vows that kept resurfacing in the quiet aftermath of those hardest moments:

"*I promise to live in the moments that are the best of us.*"

At first, that line felt accusatory. How could I live in the best of us when I felt like the worst of myself? But eventually, I understood something I hadn't before. The best of us wasn't a feeling, it was a choice.

It was choosing to walk back into the nursery after stepping away.

Choosing to pick her back up.

Choosing to fight self-pity because self-pity would render me useless—and my wife and daughter needed me to show up.

I was not at my best but they still deserved everything I could give.

And even in the middle of anger, jealousy, exhaustion, and doubt, I was still giving. That mattered more than how I felt in any single moment.

I thought fatherhood would test my patience. I didn't expect it to test my identity. I believed being a good father meant never feeling anger, never wanting space, never doubting myself.

What I learned instead was this:

Emotions are involuntary.

Actions are chosen.

Feeling anger did not make me unsafe.

Feeling jealousy did not make me disloyal.

Wanting space did not make me disconnected.

Quitting would have – and I never quit.

The father I imagined never felt doubt.

The father I became felt everything.

And that didn't make him worse.

It made him real.

Chapter 10

Coming Up for Air – When the Fog Lifted

There was a distinct morning when I realized my mind was back. It wasn't dramatic. There was no trumpet fanfare or cinematic swell of music. It was simply the third restful night in a row. I woke up and felt intact.

My thoughts were crisp—not frantic, not foggy. Clear. The high-level cognitive functions that had quietly gone offline during those first months were back online. I could feel the difference immediately. Small tasks that had required deliberate effort—assembling a bottle, organizing the diaper station, remembering which load of laundry was mid-cycle—had returned to muscle memory. My brain was no longer allocating nearly all of its capacity to survival.

And with that clarity came something even more noticeable: patience.

The same minor moments of fuss that once triggered the pounding in my ears and the tingling in my fingertips barely registered. They weren't gone. Nora still cried. She still protested naps. She was still a baby. But my nervous system no longer interpreted every cry as a threat to sustainability.

The crisis had never been the crying. It had been the belief that I could not endure it.

And now, I knew I could.

Relief came first—not subtle relief, but overwhelming relief. The kind that makes you exhale deeply without realizing you'd been holding your breath for months. Then pride.

We had survived something aggressive and complex in an incredibly short amount of time. In just a few months, I had dismantled and rebuilt my entire self-image while still showing up every day for my family. The version of me who once questioned whether he was built for fatherhood had quietly evolved into someone who understood that fatherhood isn't something you simply "are." It's something you choose—daily.

We made it intact as a family. That mattered more than any sleep metric, feeding schedule, or parenting strategy ever could.

There were moments during those early months when all I could do was sit beside Kate while she fed and held Nora. No physical task. No logistical checklist. Nothing to fix. Just presence.

At the time, it felt insufficient. Passive. I wasn't rocking, swaddling, troubleshooting, or solving anything. I was simply there. Now, with clearer eyes, I sometimes wonder: Did I do that more for myself, or for them? Was I showing up because I needed to feel useful? Or did it matter to Kate to know she would never have to endure those long feeds alone?

The honest answer is probably both.

And I've come to believe that both is enough.

Showing up doesn't always look like solving. Sometimes it looks like staying. Sometimes it looks like sitting quietly in a room that feels overwhelming and refusing to leave someone alone inside it. In those moments, I wasn't ineffective. I was steady. And steadiness is its own form of strength.

As the fog lifted, something else shifted too. My expectations of myself stopped being rigid and started becoming directional. Before Nora was born, I had a fixed image of the father I would be—calm, capable, exceptional in every moment. When reality challenged that image, I interpreted the gap as failure.

Now I see it differently.

My vision for myself isn't someone I must be every second. It's someone I strive to be every day.

Identity is not a static performance standard. It's a daily decision. It has to adapt to the needs of my family, the realities of the season we're in, and my own capacity as a human being. There will be more sleepless nights.

More developmental shifts. More seasons where I feel stretched thin. But difficulty no longer feels like disqualification.

I don't need to eliminate doubt to be a good father. I need to show up despite it.

If you are in the fog right now—if your heart pounds heavier than you expected, if you feel jealousy you didn't anticipate, if you question your capacity in the quiet hours of the night—know this: the emotion is not the verdict. The moment is not the identity.

You are not broken because this feels harder than you imagined. You are evolving. And evolution is rarely comfortable.

The first three months did not turn me into the father I expected. They introduced me to the father I am choosing to become.

Fatherhood, I've learned, is not a fixed role you step into fully formed. It is a series of decisions made in exhaustion, in doubt, in love, in fear, and in clarity. It is the quiet discipline of showing up when you are unsure and the humility of adjusting when you are wrong. It is not about eliminating struggle. It is about continuing despite it.

And in that continuation, something unexpected happens. The choice stops feeling like survival and starts feeling like stewardship. You begin to understand that the opportunity to choose your family—again and again—is not a burden.

It is a privilege.

And tomorrow, I get to choose it again.

About the Author

Long Dao wrote *The Father I Thought I'd Be* after discovering that the first three months of fatherhood were far more emotionally complex than he had ever been prepared for. What began as a personal attempt to make sense of exhaustion, frustration, guilt, and self-doubt became a book for fathers who need permission to feel what they feel without judging themselves for it. He hopes his story helps new parents feel seen, understood, and a little less alone.

www.ingramcontent.com/pod-product-compliance
Lightning Source LLC
LaVergne TN
LVHW010546100826
845148LV00013B/2627